CREATURES OF THE WILD

WOLF

GENERAL EDITOR:
ANN MALLARD
DEPARTMENT OF BIOLOGY, CITY COLLEGE OF SAN FRANCISCO

PHOTOGRAPHY BY
ALAN AND SANDY CAREY

GREENWICH EDITIONS

This edition first published in 1998 by
PRC Publishing Ltd.
Kiln House
210 New Kings Road
London SW6 4NZ

Produced for Greenwich Editions

Bibliophile House

10, Blenheim Court, Brewery Road

London, N7 9NT

This edition was produced by American Graphic Systems, Inc., in cooperation with the
Northwest Natural History Society (NWNHS).
Design © 1998 American Graphic Systems, Inc.
Designed and captioned by Bill Yenne
with design assistance by Azia Yenne

All photographs are © 1998 Alan and Sandy Carey

We are grateful for the information provided for this book by the US Fish & Wildlife Service.

Note on terminology: According to the United States Endangered Species Act, the term "endangered" means a species is considered in danger of extinction throughout all or a significant portion of its range, while "threatened" is a less dire category, meaning a species is considered likely to become endangered, but not in danger of extinction.

ISBN 0 86288 1722

Printed and bound in China

WOLF

GENERAL EDITOR:

ANN MALLARD

DEPARTMENT OF BIOLOGY, CITY COLLEGE OF SAN FRANCISCO

The call of the wild of which Jack London wrote was actually the call of the wolf, and as such, the wolf has come to symbolize the very essence of North America's wilderness. Sometimes referred to as the timber wolf, North America's gray wolf (*Canis lupus*) is the continent's largest canine carnivore. It is a near cousin to the domestic dog (*Canis familiaris*), which is thought to have evolved from the wolf or from a common ancestor. The dog has been domesticated for thousands of years and has been useful to humans in many ways, such as for transportation of goods, guarding of livestock, and protection.

Today many are kept by humans simply for companionship. Although they are a separate species, dogs are known to successfully hybridize with wolves, and the offspring are fertile. Coyotes, (*Canis latrans*) are also closely related. They are considerably smaller than wolves; they do not hunt in packs, and generally they compete with wolves — although they take smaller prey. Coyotes can be distinguished on sight from both wolves and large dogs because coyotes carry their tails low when they run, whereas wolves and dogs hold their tails high. However, lone wolves separate from their packs have been known to hybridize with coyotes, and recent genetic studies show a surprising amount of similarity in their DNA indicating that these two species are more closely related than we had previously thought.

Wolves and their relatives are members of the family Canidae, or canines, which are, in turn, part of the order Carnivora, the carnivores or meat eaters. Canidae incorporates 36 species, which are widely distributed, occurring on all continents except Antarctica. Indeed, Canids include the only carnivorous mammals to occur naturally in Australia. This animal is the dingo, which is thought to have been introduced by humans during prehistoric times. Fossil records of the Canidae date back to the Oligocene and the Miocene, making them one of the oldest extant groups of carnivores.

In addition to wolves (*Canis lupus*), dogs (*Canis familiaris*), and coyotes (*Canis latrans*), the worldwide family of Canines includes the Arctic fox (*Alopex lagopus*), the jackal (*Canis aureus*), the dingo (*Canis familiaris dingo*), the red wolf (*Canis rufus*), the Ethiopian wolf (*Canis simensis*), the crab-eating fox (*Cerdocyon thous*), the maned fox (*Chrysocyon brachyurus*), the dhole (*Cuon alpinus*), the African hunting dog (*Lycaon pictus*), the bat-eared fox (*Otocyon megalotis*), the gray fox (*Urocyon cinereoargenteus*), the African pale fox (*Vulpes pallida*) and the red fox (*Vulpes vulpes*).

Though mainly meat eaters, canids are more omnivorous than many carnivores, eating invertebrates, plants, and carrion, as well as the prey they kill themselves. Adapted more for endurance than for speed, they catch prey by pursuit over long distances in relatively open terrain until the prey tires. Kills are made by grabbing for the nape of the neck and tackling the prey to the ground. The neck grab is followed by a violent shake, which can dislocate the neck of the prey. Sense of smell is very important and well developed, as is hearing, but sight is less developed.

Some canids, especially wolves, form packs, which allow them to capture species much larger than themselves. Packs have strict social hierarchies that, in wolves, allow mating to occur only between the two dominant individuals in the pack. Pack-forming species, as well as species such as foxes, are very territorial. Territory marking occurs in many species through repeated urination on objects on the periphery of and within territories.

Although the dog is commonly considered to be "man's best friend," many canids are viewed as pests to humans, and many species have been

Opposite: The call of the wild of which Jack London wrote was actually the call of the wolf.

harmed by hunting. Coyotes and wolves are both persecuted by ranchers, who blame them for losses to sheep and cattle herds or poultry. Other species, such as foxes, have been targeted as carriers of rabies and have been the target of extermination efforts..Some foxes are valued for their pelts, which have been used in the fashion industry.

Wolves reached North America across the Bering land bridge early in the Ice Age when it was revealed by a falling sea level. The gray wolf goes by many common names, such as timber wolf, lobo, prairie wolf, and so on, but at present there are considered to be only two species of wolf throughout the world: the gray wolf, *Canis lupus*, which ranged through most of North America, Europe and Asia, and the red wolf, *Canis rufus*, which once lived in the southeastern United States, but which is now on the edge of extinction. The gray wolf is sometimes divided into 24 different subspecies. However this number may be reduced to five.

Scientists believe that Eurasian and American wolves always remained in contact, and hence part of the same gene pool. For this reason, it is generally accepted that the two groups have not evolved separately for long enough to become distinct species.

One of the most curious of the *Canis lupus* subspecies is the Japanese wolf (*Canis lupus hodophilax*), a miniature of the gray wolf family, and the smallest wolf in the world. Although the Japanese wolf is a tiny dog-like creature, human fear and misunderstanding of it led to its being both feared and revered. Because of this, throughout history it was bestowed many common names, such as okami (great god), magami (true god) and yama no kami (mountain god). The Japanese wolf was indigenous to the islands of Honshu, Shikoku and Kyushu, where it roamed the remote mountainous areas. Its small, well proportioned frame was perfectly adapted to living in the rugged, heavily forested mountain terrain.

Besides the gray wolf, (*Canis lupus*) there is one other distinct North American wolf subspecies: the Mexican wolf (*Canis lupus baileyi*). The Mexican wolf occurred in the southern part of the North American continent, overlapping the range of the red wolf (*Canis rufus*), and both of these ani-

Opposite: Though vulnerable, the pups display the alertness and curiosity that will be important qualities as they mature. Wolf pups, of which a half dozen or more are often born in a litter, are usually raised communally by the pack.

mals, the Mexican wolf and the red wolf, have come perilously close to extinction. They are discussed separately, below.

Gray wolves and people evolved in the Ice Age in Eurasia and spread throughout a large part of the world in each other's company. Though they were often in conflict, the relationship between wolves and humans was governed by mutual tolerance and respect. Most Native Americans and Inuit people (Eskimos), who retained the hunting lifestyle far longer than most cultures, revered the gray wolf, trying to emulate its cunning and hunting abilities. Like many Native Americans, the Anishinabe or Ojibwa of present-day Michigan consider themselves spiritually more closely connected to the wolf than to any other creature. According to their creation story, in "the beginning" the wolf and the man were brothers. The original man and his brother Maengun, the wolf, traveled together to name and visit all the plants, animals, and places on earth. Later, they were instructed by the Creator to walk their separate paths and that they both would be feared, respected and misunderstood by the people that would join them on earth.

Opposite: Seasonal change is characteristic of the wolf's habitat. The wolf is at home throughout the northern tier of the United States and Canada, although its range once included all of North America.

FAMILY CANIDAE ADULT WEIGHT COMPARISONS
Pounds (Kilograms in parentheses)

Gray wolf (*Canis lupus*)		
	Low average	60(27)
	High average	130(60)
Red wolf (*Canis rufus*)		
	Low average	45(20)
	High average	80(36)
Coyote (*Canis latrans*)		
	Low average	20(9)
	High average	50(23)
Red fox (*Vulpes vulpes*)		
	Low average	8(4)
	High average	15(7)

Many Native American clans were identified with animals, such as the bear or the eagle, and almost always the wolf was a totem animal. This meant members of the wolf clan derived strength and gained protection from the wolf, but that they could not kill it. Many of the creation myths of the North American Indian tribes focused on the paradox that man has always seen in the wolf: we feel a natural kinship with the wolf as a social animal which looks after its own in the pack, and a natural fear (or is it admiration?) of the wolf as a large and dangerous predator.

The wolf was once common to most of the Northern Hemisphere, with a range that included most of the United States, Europe and the Middle East. But attitudes towards the wolf changed as humans ceased to be hunter-gatherers and adopted agricultural lifestyles and domesticated the wolf's cousin, the dog. In Europe a much darker imagery grew up around wolves. They were consistently the villains in werewolf myths and fairy tales, and Europeans saw nothing admirable in wolves. Of course Europe was much more closely settled than North America, so that wolves and men were bound to come into conflict before firearms were common. During the great wars of Europe, when hundreds of dead were left on the battlefields, the wolves would come to feed on the carcasses. Such wolves developed a taste for human flesh and there are accounts of wolves entering into towns and attacking people during the Middle Ages. In 1439 wolves are reported to have eaten four women in Paris. So some of the wolf horror stories were based on fact, but the fictions also proliferated, and when Europeans settled in North America they brought their fear and hatred of the wolf with them.

Second only to humans in its adaptation to climate extremes, the gray wolf was once equally at home in the deserts of the Middle East, the deciduous forests of Virginia, and the frozen Arctic of Siberia. The last wolves were exterminated in the British Isles in the eighteenth century. By the twentieth century, wolves had disappeared from most of Western Europe and Japan. Remnants of wolf populations still exist in Poland, Scandinavia, Russia, Portugal, Spain, and Italy. While the gray wolf formerly ranged over the greater part of the North American continent, it was most abundant in the Great Plains. When the buffalo herds in countless thousands were seeking new pastures, the gray wolf flourished, preying on the newly born calves, as well as feeble, wounded, or aged buffalo. Today they are found only in the far north of the United States and the remotest corners of Europe, but they are present in almost all of Canada except the Maritime provinces.

Within North America, the habitat of the wolf is also incredibly varied, probably depending more on prey than on the cover or comfort provided by vegetation or landform. Wolves choose home territories in forests and meadows, in mountains with rocky ridges, lakes or rivers, in the great plains or on the tundra of the far north. In the West, wolves have been known to follow the seasonal movements of elk or buffalo herds, but in central Alaska, wolves don't follow migrating moose or caribou outside their pack territories.

A pack uses a distinct territory, which it defends against other packs, but during the winter, wolves may travel long distances, especially when the main prey is a migratory animal, such as the caribou. Wolves need a large, remote area relatively free from human disturbance where they live in packs of two to 20, depending on the physical size of available prey. Where deer are the main

Opposite: The wolf pack on the move amid the winter snows. For wolves, it was through the controversial practice of reintroduction into environments from which they were purposely exterminated.

prey, packs number from five to 10 wolves, but when the prey is large, like moose or caribou, packs are larger, and also territories. Each pack has a territory that is marked and defended. Sizes of individual wolf pack territories reported from the Great Lakes area ranged from 30 to 260 square miles, but average approximately 100 square miles in Wisconsin and Minnesota. However, one pack of five animals monitored in the Upper Peninsula in 1992-1993 used an area of 310 square miles. In the Arctic, where the prey is musk ox and snowshoe hares, a pack may cover several thousand square miles, and on Ellesmere Island one pack covered 5,000 square miles in only six weeks! Territory size fluctuates each season, depending on the size of the pack and the number of prey.

Wolves are large in comparison to coyotes, with body dimensions exceeding those of a fully grown German shepherd or Alaskan malamute. Male wolves are slightly larger than females. Weights of adult gray wolves range from 60-115 pounds and average about 75 pounds, but there is a lot of variation— the largest wolf taken in Alaska weighed 175 pounds. Gray

Opposite: Wolves now roam a larger part of the northern United States than they did in the middle twentieth century, including Montana's Flathead River drainage (seen here) and Michigan's Upper Peninsula.

FAMILY CANIDAE ADULT HEIGHT COMPARISONS

Inches (centimeters in parentheses)

Gray wolf (*Canis lupus*)		
	Low average	24(60)
	High average	36(90)
Red wolf (*Canis rufus*)		
	Low average	24(60)
	High average	32(80)
Coyote (*Canis latrans*)		
	Low average	24(60)
	High average	26(65)
Red fox (*Vulpes vulpes*)		
	Low average	14(35)
	High average	18(45)

wolves are about six feet long from nose to the end of the tail. Adults stand 26 -38 inches tall at the shoulder, but Mexican wolves and red wolves are considerably smaller.

Gray wolves vary widely in appearance. They are often pure white and more slight of build in the Arctic, while in the taiga or northern forests of Canada and the United States they are larger and dark gray or black. However, there are also pale gray wolves and cream or tan wolves with brindled backs. In cold climates the dense underfur in their winter coats is protected by guard hairs which may be up to six inches long over the shoulder. The feet of wolves are large, with tracks measuring 3-4 inches wide and 4-5 inches long — nearly as large as the palm of a human hand. Wolves have cheek tufts that make their faces appear wide and their heads large. Their tails are bushy and straight, not curled like most dogs'.

Wolves are among the most social of carnivores. The pack is the functional unit of wolf society, and the animals within the pack depend on cooperation for survival. A pack is typically comprised of two lead or, "alpha," animals, the current year's pups, siblings from previous litters, and occasionally other wolves that may or may not be related to the alpha pair. The alpha male and female normally are the only animals that breed, even though other pack members are physiologically capable of reproduction. The alpha animals are thought to lead in decisions such as when and where to hunt and when it is time to move, rest, or find seclusion. The alpha female is believed to select the denning site. Much of the time that the pack spends together is used to reinforce the intricate dominance hierarchy within the pack through structured greetings and body posturings. The alpha pair always takes the first food from a kill. Wolves which are subordinate to the alpha pair, approach them with their heads low, and their tails between their legs. Or they roll over and present their bellies or groin areas to be sniffed. Even from the air the dominance hierarchy of a pack can be viewed as the wolves often travel single file,

Opposite: Rather than being turned out by their mother, as occurs with other species, many wolf pups will be integrated into the life of their parents' pack.

FAMILY CANIDAE ADULT LENGTH COMPARISONS
Inches (centimeters in parentheses)

Gray wolf (*Canis lupus*)		
	Low average	60(150)
	High average	72(180)
Red wolf (*Canis rufus*)		
	Low average	42(105)
	High average	60(150)
Coyote (*Canis latrans*)		
	Low average	42(105)
	High average	54(135)
Red fox (*Vulpes vulpes*)		
	Low average	36(90)
	High average	42(105)

the alpha pair carrying their tails high, while the subordinate wolves are holding their tails appropriately lower.

The hierarchy within a pack changes as some wolves age, or get sick, and younger ones gain in strength and maturity. Old dominants may become subordinates, or they may be chased out of a pack. Then they become dispersers, or lone wolves, often travelling hundreds of miles, hoping to find another pack or a new territory to find a mate and start their own pack. One such wolf moved 550 miles, from south of International Falls, Minnesota to eastern Saskatchewan. It is in this way that new packs have recently been formed in the northern United States by dispersers from Canada.

Pack life centers largely around mating, which takes place in midwinter, usually in February. In fact much of the dominance hierarchy is actually based on reproductive rights — who is allowed to mate and reproduce. Females usually become sexually mature at about 22 months. Although only the alpha pair will reproduce, subordinate males may mate with the alpha female before she becomes fertile. As her time of ovulation approaches, the alpha male becomes very protective and aggressive towards all other subordinate wolves. Subordinate females who are mature enough to bear young appear to be inhibited from becoming fertile — perhaps by stress from the increased dominance of the alpha pair. This pair forms a strong bond and are often lifelong mates. After mating, they withdraw from the pack to den together.

Wolves often build their dens in well-drained soils in meadows near water, and they may use the same den for several years. Wolves also den under tree roots, rock outcrops, hollow logs, or even in former beaver lodges. Dens are usually dug by early March. Gestation lasts 60 to 63 days, and pups are born in late April. Litter sizes range from one to nine pups, but average four to six.

The pups are born blind and depend completely on their mother's milk for the first month. They are weaned at about five weeks and moved to a rendezvous site (a meadow or an open area in the forest) at about eight weeks. Now the pack will reassemble as all pack members feed and care for the pups. Indeed, the whole group assists in the upbringing, acting as baby sitters when the mother herself goes hunting, and guarding the area from predators, such as grizzly bears. This activity strengthens the social bonds among pack members, which is critical for their survival as communal hunters. As the pups grow, they are fed partially digested food brought to the den or rendezvous site and regurgitated from the stomachs of returning adults. During the summer, the pack may change its rendezvous site several times. By the end of summer, the pups are beginning to hunt with the adults, and the pack is once more able to be on the move.

Wolves are among the best examples in the animal world of population self-regulation, limiting production of pups by allowing only the alpha pair to breed. Litter sizes for wolves also vary, with larger litters being born when prey is abundant, while during lean years the pack may not breed at all. There is about 60 percent mortality for pups and young wolves. Death is usually caused by starvation or disease, but also by battles between wolf packs or from predation by bears. Adult wolves live for eight or nine years in the wild. Adult

Opposite: A gray wolf on the move against the spectacular backdrop of the Montana Rockies.

wolves are not attacked by any predators, besides man. The main causes of death are accidents, malnutrition, starvation, parasites, diseases, and fatal encounters during territorial disputes between packs, or with man.

Because they live in packs, wolves are able to cooperate when they hunt prey larger than themselves, such as elk, deer, and moose, or in the far north, caribou, reindeer and musk ox. Before the late nineteenth century, the buffalo was a key source of food for wolves living on the Great Plains of North America. Other large prey include pronghorn and bighorn sheep. When hunting larger prey, wolves seek out the weak and vulnerable, the young of the year and the old or sick. A wolf can consume up to 20 pounds of meat at one meal, and usually utilizes the entire carcass, including some hair and bones. Wolves will also prey on game birds, waterfowl, rabbits and smaller mammals, such as beaver and various rodents. In Yellowstone National Park, wolves attack buffalo, and they've been known to kill black bears. Wolves also prey on domestic livestock and poultry, and of course this predation has

increased as ranches and farms have taken over the lands once used by their wild prey.

Smaller prey, such as beavers, rabbits, and other small mammals, may be a substantial part of the diet of lone wolves. Indirectly, the kills of wolves support a wide variety of other animals: ravens, foxes, wolverines, vultures, and even bears feed on the remains of animals killed by wolves. Wolf kills have also been found to be an important source of food for eagles.

When large prey, such as caribou or moose, are abundant, wolves live in larger groups to enable pack hunting. This enables them to take larger prey, and has given rise to the frightening picture of a pack of ravenous wolves terrorizing their prey and decimating their numbers. The relationship between wolves as predators and their prey was intensively studied by David Mech on Isle Royale. Isle Royal National Park was established in 1931 on an isolated island in Lake Superior primarily for the protection of the native plants and

Above: Wolves begin to mate in their second or third season of life. As with other species, this will begin with a courtship ritual, seen here, in which the male seeks to gain the favor of the female.

Above: The courtship between the male and female gray wolf involves nuzzling and various types of play that is similar to that which can be observed routinely among domestic dogs.

animals, including woodland caribou, lynx and coyotes. Moose had swum to the island in about 1912 and their population numbers had exploded. Then in 1948 a single pair of wolves crossed an ice bridge to the island, creating a great opportunity to study the relationship between predators and prey in a closed system. Mech's long-term studies at Isle Royale proved that, at least in the Isle Royale system, wolves did not actually regulate the numbers of their prey — the numbers of both predators and prey were regulated by the amount of food available, especially in winter.

However, they did act as an effective population control by taking the weakest members of the herd, the calves, and the older moose which were sick with disease. Many moose get an infestation of ticks and hydatids which cause cysts in their lungs, so that they can hardly breathe. Such animals are natural prey for the wolves, and predation by wolves is a natural way of culling out the unhealthy animals in the moose population. However, even in

Above: A courting couple will occasionally share a howl together. Howling, a wolf habit long known, but little understood, is observed to occur often during wintertime mating rituals.

Above: An appearance of affection between a courting pair. Some gray wolves, such as these, are a true gray color, while others, such as those on the opposite page, are distinctly golden.

their attacks on the weaker animals of a herd, the cooperative hunting tech-
niques of a pack are the most effective way to bring down such large prey as a
moose, which may weigh in at 1,000 pounds, easily 10 times the weight of
one wolf. Even a pack of wolves has a hard time bringing down such large
prey — they are not able to simply take a larger animal such as a moose or a
deer any time they feel hungry (as a man might do armed with a rifle). In fact
Mech's studies showed that wolves approach about twelve deer or moose for
every one they actually catch.

A formal monitoring program of the moose and wolves on Isle Royale
began in 1958. Wolf numbers have varied between 12 and 50; moose numbers, from 500 to 1,900. The wolf and moose populations on the island followed a pattern of dynamic fluctuations, wherein high moose numbers (par-
ticularly numbers of older moose) were followed by higher wolf numbers.
Wolves influenced moose numbers predominantly through the direct killing

Above: A group of wolf pups emerge
from their den. A typical litter will
number about six pups, who will be
born in late spring. They are usually
darker in color than they will be as
adults.

Above: This mother is in the process of digging a den for the birth of her pups. The den, which is often reused, can be an elaborate underground structure with several rooms.

of calves and have remained the only consistent source of moose mortality on the island. The moose-wolf population patterns held until a dramatic crash occurred in the wolf population in the early 1980s, in which wolf numbers dropped from 50 to 14.

This population crash was circumstantially linked to an introduction of canine parvovirus enteritis disease. As the moose population grew throughout the 1980s and 1990s, the wolf population failed to correspondingly increase. Intensive research initiated in 1988 focused on other possible causes for the wolf decline: food shortage, disease, and genetic problems. It is quite possible that wolf numbers are dropping due to overall weakness caused by inbreeding and compounded by disease. Researchers have estimated that there has been a 50 percent loss of genetic variability in the isolated population of Isle Royale wolves, and wolf reproduction has progressively declined since 1985. Currently there are only 14 wolves remaining on the island, which is far below the

Above: A pair of pups relaxes with their alert and attentive mother. The young are weaned at about 30 days, but continue to depend upon adults for their solid food.

Above: The proud mother and her doting pup. The pups will emerge from the den fairly soon after birth, but they will continue to spend their nights there for about six weeks.

number which could be supported based on the size of the moose population. A possible outcome is a complete die-off of the Isle Royale wolf population.

Humans understand their world mainly through sight and communicate with words. Wolves have good eyesight, but they read the world and communicate most extensively through their sense of smell — probably their most acute sense. The pack delineates its territory, and the individual marks his presence by placing scent marks, especially urine or scat. Scat may bear the odor of hormone secretions from the anal glands. Wolves also scratch the ground to leave both a visual and an olfactory mark of their presence. Thus, the entire territory of a pack is marked — the trails and rendezvous sites, as well as the boundaries — and a wolf travelling through it will be able to read the signs and know who passed that way recently, and perhaps even what mood it was in.

Above: These pups, though still quite dark, are already displaying the patterns of color they will have as adults. Wolves are born dark and almost always become lighter.

Above: These wolf pups, though from the same litter, are quite different in color. The one on the ground is much lighter than a typical pup, while the black one may well remain that color when it matures.

Wolves also communicate vocally, using whines and whimpers, growls, barks and howls. Whines are plaintive begging sounds, and they may indicate pain, but they are also used by pupus or subordinate wolves towards a dominant adult. Growling indicates anger or aggression. Usually it is directed at another wolf and may begin a dominance fight. A bark seems to be a warning; it is often used by an adult disciplining pups. And of course, wolves howl.

Anyone who has heard the sound of a wolf howling in the northern woods by night will agree that the wolf howl is the most enigmatic and fascinating of all the noises made by wolves — or perhaps of all the noises heard in the wild. For some humans it is the voice of the wilderness. For others it is the sound of evil which strikes a chord of fear and hatred. The noise itself is very complex, a long, drawn-out, continuous sound, with one fundamental tone overlaid with two or three related harmonic tones. Wolves most commonly howl in the late evening or early morning. They never yap in combi-

Above: The wolf pups will play near the den through the summer, growing and exploring their world.

Above: During their playful first summer, the pups will learn the social skills that will be essential to their life as adults, when they must interact as members of a pack.

nation with their howls, as coyotes do. Howling is much more common during the mating season, in midwinter, and during the raising of pups at the rendezvous sites in midsummer. There is less howling in early spring, probably in an effort to protect the den site. In spite of many studies, biologists are still not sure why wolves howl. It is thought that howling is used for gathering the pack together before a hunt and for territorial announcements to other packs — but it remains a fascinating mystery to man.

In recent years, biologists have learned to use howling to study wolves. The researcher can howl out into the night and the wolves will answer. Surely they must know that this is not another wolf, but for some reason, they enjoy the game. The researcher gets information about the whereabouts and even the numbers of packs much more easily than he would be able to by walking the woods and reading the signs of tracks. Howling has also become a tourist attraction at several parks in Canada, and at the International Wolf

Above: As the pups grow, their caregivers gradually give them more and more latitude in how far they are allowed to venture from the den in their explorations.

Above: Relationships formed between pups will continue to be important as they grow into adults and take on important roles within the pack.

Center near Ely in Minnesota. The practice began in Canada at Algonquin Provincial Park in 1963, when park officials asked biologists who were surveying wolf populations if they would give a demonstration of howling and allow the visitors to hear the response. Ever since, wolf howls have been held occasionally in Canadian parks, and in 1990, 1,600 people attended each of two wolf howls. There were over a thousand people at night under the stars listening for wolves, and you could hear a pin drop.

While their cousin, the dog, is considered to be "man's best friend," the wolf has always been at odds with humans. European settlers brought with them a deep fear and hatred of wolves developed over many years of conflict in Europe. Then, as they moved west across the virgin lands of North America, they severely depleted most populations of bison, deer, elk, and moose — the animals that were important prey for wolves. The wolf then turned to the sheep and cattle that people had introduced to replace its natural prey. With

Above: The family instinct and bond between parents and pups is very strong among gray wolves. As with most mammals, the mother is jealously protective of her young.

the coming of the railroads, ranching became big business, and to protect their livestock, ranchers and government agencies began a campaign to eliminate the wolf. Bounty programs, initiated in the nineteenth century, continued as late as 1965, offering up to $20 to $50 per wolf. Wolves were trapped, shot from planes and snowmobiles, and hunted with dogs. Animal carcasses salted with strychnine were left out for wolves to eat and the poisoned wolves could be submitted for bounties. Unfortunately, this practice also indiscriminately killed eagles, ravens, foxes, bears, and other animals which also fed on the poisoned carrion. As the war against the wolf gained momentum, some of the tactics used became quite diabolical. In the early twentieth century a law was passed in Montana requiring the state veterinarian to inoculate captured wolves with sarcoptic mange and then turn them loose to spread the disease.

It was the belief of settlers in the American West that the wolf caused widespread livestock losses and cost them millions of dollars a year. In 1915

Above: The adults of the pack all cooperate in teaching the pups the many aspects of behavior that will help them to survive and flourish when they mature.

Above: The mother will take primary responsibility for the pups in her litter, but the females of the pack will take turns hunting and babysitting the pups.

the United States Congress authorized funding to totally eradicate wolves on all public lands. This led to the establishment of PARC, the Predatory Animal and Rodent Control Service, which employed wolf hunters to trap and kill the wolves.

Under large-scale predator control programs, wolves were hunted and killed with more passion and zeal than any other animal in United States history. To make the bitter tasting strychnine poison more palatable the PARC hunters molded it into balls of fat from the back of a horse or cow and scattered the baits near wolf trails. Thus they killed all the remaining wolves in Texas and Arizona (as well as a lot of other wildlife). New and tasteless poisons were developed after World War II, when "wolf control" was taken over by US Fish and Wildlife Service. However, by this time the wolf was nearly extinct throughout most of North America south of Canada.

Above: A young wolf snuggles with his mother, who is dozing peacefully after nursing. This pup is quite mature and is probably within one or two feedings of being weaned.

Above: A mother wolf nurses a growing pup. When they were young, the mother could easily nurse her entire litter. At this age, only one can be accommodated easily.

In the United States, the wolf was exterminated from all the lower 48 states except Minnesota and the upper peninsula of Michigan, and possibly northern Idaho, Montana and Wyoming. None of these were resident wolves. They were loners, dispersers and wanderers. Possibly more in the realm of myth, there have been undocumented sightings of lone wolves from the mountainous regions of New Mexico, Arizona and Colorado.

Today, wolves generally are classified as big game and furbearers in Canada and Alaska, as a threatened species in Minnesota, and as an endangered species elsewhere in the lower 48 states. In many parts of the world, the gray wolf, according to the IUCN (International Union for the Conservation of Nature), is classified as "vulnerable to extinction." In France and Spain, as well as in North America, there are efforts being made toward species recovery. However, in Russia, Romania and the Scandinavian countries the wolf populations are not receiving the same level of protection.

Above: The pup appears oblivious to his mother's howl. Wolves howl more frequently in the evening and early morning.

Opposite: A pup imitating his mother's howl.

In North America the tide began to turn in favor of the wolf in the 1970s, when it was first declared an endangered species in 1973, and then again when this was clarified in 1978 by listing the Minnesota population as threatened. The changing attitudes towards wolves can be tracked in the Upper Peninsula of Michigan. Here bounty records show that there were 30 wolves bountied in 1956, and one in 1959. In 1960 Michigan repealed the bounty, and in 1965 granted the wolf full protection by law.

State protection was soon followed by federal protection under the Endangered Species Act. Wolves began to colonize Glacier National Park in the 1970s and the first wolf den in the western United States. in over 50 years was documented there in 1986. Since then the Glacier population has increased to 50 or 60 animals, and wolves dispersing from here have established five other packs elsewhere in Montana. Biologists were able to verify the existence of ever-increasing numbers of single animals in Wisconsin and

Above: Female gray wolves have their first litter at age two or three, and mate each year thereafter, usually with the same male if he is still alive and a member of the pack.

Above: A mother and her pup take a break from hunt training. By the time they are eight months old, most of the young wolves have been taught how to hunt.

in the Upper Peninsula of Michigan, and finally in the spring of 1991, a verified pair of wolves travelling together in the central Upper Peninsula produced pups for the first time in recent memory.

Today, wolves are making a strong comeback in many areas of the lower
48 states, as packs move south out of Canada. They are recolonizing northern
Washington, as well as Idaho and Montana, from stable populations in Canada, while wolves are moving from Minnesota into Wisconsin and Michigan.

In Minnesota, where the largest wolf population in the lower 48 states
resides, a special state program provides compensation for livestock confirmed
to be killed by wolves, and a federal program provides for trapping of individual wolves guilty of killing livestock. The Minnesota wolves, thought to be an
extension of the Ontario population, number between 1,550 and 2,000.
About 60 to 70 live in Michigan's Upper Peninsula, about 55 in Wisconsin,
and nearly 100 in Montana.

Above: A gangly young wolf nuzzles his
mother. Just as in humans, the hair
color of the mother does not necessari-
ly determine the hair color of the pup.

Above: This all-black pup is about eight months old and is ready to take his place among his parents' generation in hunting for food and defending the pack.

Numbers are low but unknown in Idaho and Washington, and an occasional individual is seen in Wyoming, North Dakota, and South Dakota. In fact, the isolated Isle Royale ecosystem represents the only place in North America where the wolf has declined dramatically in the 1980s and 1990s.

Populations fluctuate throughout the world due to food availability and strife within packs. In Canada, up to 58,000 gray wolves occur in about 80 percent of their former range. In Alaska, 5,200 to 7,200 wolves live on most of their original range on about 84 percent of the state's area. Outside of North America, there are about 30,000 in Russia (mainly in Siberia) and about 5,000 in Europe, half of these in Romania.

Above: A pair of yearling pups engaged in play.

Above: The innocent-faced pups grow into adults, whose piercing visage is all business. Keen senses of hearing and smell are vitally important during the hunt.

THE MEXICAN WOLF

Unlike the red wolf (*Canis rufus*), the Mexican wolf (*Canis lupus baileyi*) is considered to be a subspecies of the gray wolf (*Canis lupus*). Like the red wolf it is considerably smaller, averaging 50 to 90 pounds, with a coat that is reddish brown in color. It originally ranged through the more mountainous areas of northern Mexico (3,000 to 12,000 feet), and into southern Arizona and New Mexico. This area is mostly dry, chaparral scrub, although the higher elevations are forested with spruce and fir, and these areas are preferred by the wolves. These wolves will cross desert areas, but do not actually live in them.

The status of the Mexican wolf in Mexico is uncertain, but very few are thought to remain in the wild, and the existence of viable wild populations is extremely unlikely. The Mexican wolf is considered to be extinct in the wild

Above: Though most gray wolves are dark at birth, some remain virtually solid black through adulthood. This coloration is less common than the typical gray with white highlights, but it is by no means rare.

Above: This striking photograph is like an illustration from a
medieval folk tale about encountering fierce wolves in a forest on a
cold and snowy day.

in the United States, with the last known wolf being taken in 1970. Like the gray wolf, it was wiped out throughout its range because it was believed that wolves were a serious threat to livestock. Since 1970, sightings of "wolves" continue to be occasionally reported from Arizona, New Mexico, and Texas, but none have been confirmed to be Mexican wolves.

In 1976, although none were known to exist in the United States, the Mexican wolf was officially listed as an endangered species under the provisions of the Endangered Species Act of 1973. Nine years later, the US Fish and Wildlife Service approved the Mexican Wolf Recovery Plan in 1982. This plan intended to establish a captive breeding program with the goal of eventually establishing a self-sustaining population in the wild within its original range, in the mountains of southern Arizona and New Mexico. Actually, most of the original habitat of this wolf was in Mexico, but it was decided that protection would be too difficult, since neither the Mexican government

Above: A group of relatively young wolves sniffs the shore of a stream for the scent of deer who may have paused here for a sip.

Above: A gray wolf pair crossing a stream. Though hunting in a pack is typical, pairs, often breeding pairs, will occasionally hunt together.

nor the ranchers in that area were enthusiastic. However, the Mexican authorities did cooperate to the extent that between 1977 and 1980, five Mexican wolves were removed from the wild in Mexico and placed in a captive breeding program in the United States. Captive wolves were paired for maximum breeding potential beginning in 1991.

Most of the work of captive breeding is actually being done in zoos, none of which are federally owned, operated, or supported. It is estimated that a captive population of from 200 to 300 Mexican wolves is needed to safeguard the subspecies from extinction and to provide stock for future reintroduction efforts. A suitable site for reintroduction has been found in the White Sands Missile Range in south-central New Mexico and the Apache and Gila National Forests in eastern Arizona and western New Mexico. The Mexican Wolf Recovery Plan concentrated on this breeding program and no introductions to the wild were made.

Above: The snap of the photographer's shutter catches the attention of a trio of wolves on the hunt.

Above: An adult wolf vaults a stream on the trail of an elk who recently drank at this spot. A keen sense of smell is an essential part of a wolf's adaptation to its environment.

THE RED WOLF

Above: The pack pauses for a rest. Actually, this may not be the entire pack, but a hunting party from the pack. All adults, both male and female, participate in the hunt.

The red wolf (*Canis rufus*) derives its name from the reddish color of the head, ears, and legs. However, its coloring can range from very light tan to black. Weighing 45 to 80 pounds, the red wolf is smaller than the gray wolf and larger than the coyote. The head is broader than the coyote's but more narrow than the gray wolf's. The red wolf's most distinguishing features are the long ears and legs.

The exact identity of the red wolf has been debated for decades, with some authorities considering it a species, some considering it a subspecies of the gray wolf, and some considering it a hybrid, or crossbreed, of the coyote and the gray wolf. In the wild, red wolves normally establish lifelong mates. Recent studies of the DNA of both the red wolf and the coyote indicate that

Above: A wolf pack consists of a dominant, or "alpha," pair of mated adults and their offspring, as well as other adults, including relatives of the alpha pair.

they are very closely related. Possibly the red wolf was a distinct species before its habitat and lifestyle were stressed by human settlers and deforestation in large areas of the south, which pushed the coyotes eastward. As numbers grew smaller and mates were scarce the red wolf may well have begun to hybridize with coyotes.

However, unlike coyotes, red wolves mate for life and maintain a pack structure. Red wolf packs generally use 10 to 100 square miles of habitat. Red wolf packs are smaller than those of the gray wolf, consisting of an adult pair and the young of the current and previous years. The pack uses 10 to 100 square miles of habitat. Similar to gray wolves, red wolves are very social and territorial.

They reach breeding maturity in their second or third year, and breed in February or March of each year. The female wolf, sometimes assisted by the male, finds or digs a suitable den in areas such as hollow logs, ditch banks, or

Above: A group of young gray wolves on the move. A pack can number as few as five wolves, but usually there are a dozen or more members in a pack.

Above: A pair of all-black wolves playing in the snow. Such fights among wolves will often occur over a fresh kill, or when a young male decides to challenge the alpha male for leadership of the pack.

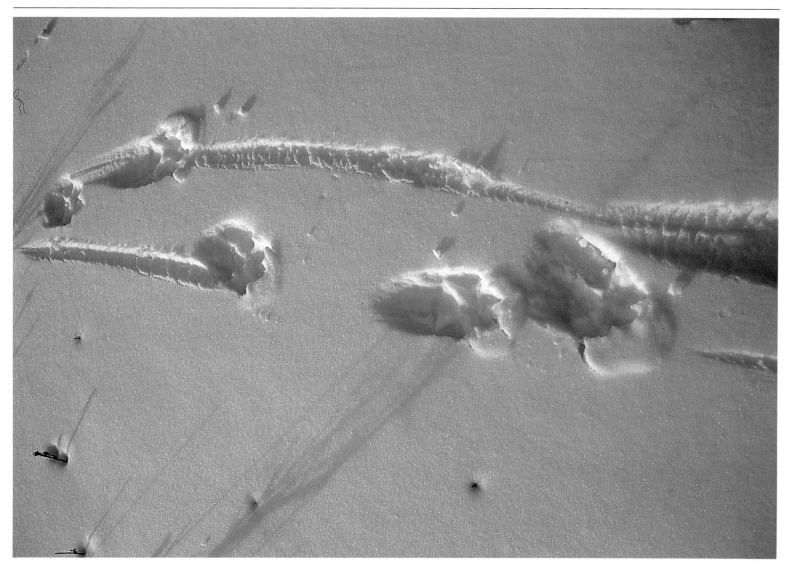

under rock outcrops. Two to six pups are born in March or April. The pups are born with their eyes closed and are completely dependent on their mother for about two months. They usually remain with the parents until reaching breeding maturity, forming small family groups, or packs.

White-tailed deer and raccoons are the most important part of the red wolf's diet, but smaller animals, such as rabbits and nutria, are eaten when available. Red wolves will prey on small livestock in certain situations, but it is believed by some that proper livestock husbandry can greatly reduce or eliminate these losses. With large livestock such as cattle, it is normally only the very young calves that are vulnerable. Yet it was the belief that the red wolf caused widespread cattle losses that led to extensive predator control programs in the early part of the twentieth century. The red wolf was also affected by land clearing and drainage projects, logging, mineral exploration, and road development that encroached on its forest habitat.

Above: Wolf tracks in the snow. Because wolves move mainly at night, one is more likely to come upon the tracks than to come upon the wolf who made them.

Above: A group of wolves at play. Such activities are not trivial, but essential in the development of the vital skills that will be needed by these wolves if they are to become successful hunters.

Originally, the red wolf roamed as far north as Pennsylvania and as far west as central Texas. Like the related gray wolf, the red wolf was eradicated from most of its former range by large scale predator control programs. By the late 1930s, only two populations are believed to have remained, one in the Ozark/Quachita Mountain region of Arkansas, Oklahoma, and Missouri, and the other in southern Louisiana and southeastern Texas. In 1967, the red wolf was listed as an endangered species (under a law that preceded the Endangered Species Act of 1973). Soon after, the US Fish & Wildlife Service established a captive breeding program for the red wolf. Biologists began to remove remaining red wolves from the wild in an effort to save the species from extinction.

By 1980, the red wolf was considered extinct in the wild. but in 1977, captive red wolf pairs had produced their first litters. Biologists took great care to maintain the wild instincts of these animals, keeping human contact to a

Above: Three wolves seize a snowshoe hare. The hare had camouflage to his advantage, but once it was detected, this was no match for the wolves' speed and strength.

Above: With prey as small as a hare, there can often be a violent disagreement among wolves over control of the prey.

minimum in order to avoid creating a dependence on man. A decade later, in 1987, four pairs of red wolves were reintroduced to the wild on the 120,000-acre Alligator River National Wildlife Refuge in northeastern North Carolina.

By the mid-1990s, there were over 50 red wolves at Alligator River. Another experimental reintroduction site was selected in the Great Smoky Mountains National Park to explore the feasibility of the red wolf's reestablishment into the Southern Appalachian Mountains. The US Fish & Wildlife Service also is working with the US Forest Service to evaluate national forest lands in the Southern Appalachians and elsewhere that may be suitable as future reintroduction sites.

By the 1990s, there were about 300 red wolves, including 220 in captivity and the rest in the wild — quite a comeback from the 14 animals making up the original captive breeding population.

Above: A pack of five feeds on the carcass of a deer. While small mammals are often eaten by wolves, deer and elk are preferred because they provide substantially more meat.

Above: A wolf in the middle of feeding can be extremely aggressive, especially with rival wolves. Such a wolf will show its fangs and snarl viciously to intimidate any animal that interferes with its meal.

WOLF RECOVERY PLANS

Because the wolf has been listed federally as an endangered species, US Fish and Wildlife is attempting various managed recovery plans as well. In central Idaho 15 wolves were reintroduced from Canada, released in January of 1995, and many of these wolves moved north, some to the Bitterroot Valley in Montana. However, it is Yellowstone National Park which has been at the center of controversy over the issue of wolf recovery.

Both Yellowstone and Glacier national parks established an official predator-control policy between 1914 and 1926 to eradicate the wolf as a danger to livestock in adjacent areas. Wolves were officially exterminated in Yellowstone by 1930 (although a lone wolf was seen in 1944), so that for 65 years, the wolf was the only traditional species missing from the Yellowstone ecosystem — one of the largest relatively intact wilderness areas in the lower

Above: A gray wolf threatening another wolf. Disagreements arise over such things as food, mating preferences and leadership. In the case of leadership, the strongest male will win the confidence of the pack.

Above: The face of the aggressive wolf has always had a place in the folklore of the Northern Hemisphere. For example, Romania, associated with legends of vampires and werewolves, actually is still home to more wolves (about 2,500) than any other country in Europe except Russia.

48 states. Since the extermination of wolves in about 1930, the population of elk and bison has risen in Yellowstone. This has led to overgrazing of Yellowstone's rangeland which, in turn, led to a reduction in the numbers of many plant and animal species that were once common there.

Some people felt that reintroduction of the wolf would complete the ecological picture. Others were concerned about potential effects on livestock and big game animals. Fear of livestock killing was the single most important cause of opposition to wolf recovery, although hunters also worried that game would be less available if wolves were to recolonize their former ranges. It was believed the large herds of elk and deer within Yellowstone would provide more than enough food for the wolves, who usually prefer wild game over livestock. However, eventually some wolves would try to live outside the park, and in other areas it was these loners who were most likely to prey on livestock.

Above: Two wary wolves look up from the carcass of a moose they have just brought down. The largest member of the deer family, a moose can provide a good meal for the whole pack.

Above: A wolf and a recently-killed moose. Wolves thrive during heavy winters, such as occur here in the Montana Rockies, because the deep snow hampers the mobility of big game such as moose.

In 1994, after years of comprehensive study and planning, the US Fish & Wildlife Service began an effort to reintroduce gray wolves into Yellowstone and adjacent US Forest Service lands in central Idaho. The Service had previously identified these areas, as well as northwest Montana, as ideal areas for wolf recovery. It was an area of natural expansion for wolf packs from Canada to expand their range.

Part of the reintroduction effort involved capturing a group of wolves from Alberta and British Columbia and bringing them to the United States for the reintroduction. When these wolves were reintroduced, they were designated as "nonessential experimental" under the Endangered Species Act. This provided for control — or killing — of wolves under certain circumstances. For example, if they were determined to be preying on livestock or if wild populations of deer, elk, and other large game were severely affected by wolves, the wolves could be shot. In the meantime, a private organization

Above: A gray wolf runs at top speed across a frozen stream. Wolves typically trot at a brisk five miles per hour, but they can run at speeds up to 45 miles per hour.

Above: A wolf dashes through the snow in pursuit of his prey. Among North American mammals, only the pronghorn antelope can outrun a wolf, and it cannot do so in deep snow.

that supported reintroduction had established a fund to compensate land owners who suffered losses to wolves.

Under the US Fish & Wildlife Service's plan for wolf recovery, reintroduction began in 1994. Wolf populations were envisioned to recover to roughly the pre-1930 level by 2002, at which time the US Fish & Wildlife Service would propose to remove the wolf in Yellowstone from the list of endangered and threatened species. Wolf recovery efforts were seen by the US Fish & Wildlife Service "to represent an opportunity to redress past mistakes and enhance our understanding, not only of the wolf itself, but also the complex interactions among species in their natural environment."

In late 1994, three acclimation pens were constructed in such places as the Lamar Valley in the northeast corner of Yellowstone. While this was being done, wolves were being captured, pre-collared and released in Alberta near Jasper National Park. There was still bitter opposition to reintroduction

Above: An alpha pair takes a break from their hunt. The alpha male and female will often hunt together, leaving their pups in the care of others.

Above: An alert wolf eyes the photographer. Wolves have no natural predators other than disease and human beings, who hunt wolves to protect their livestock.

among the ranchers and hunters, and a lawsuit was filed by the Wyoming Farm Bureau and other concerned parties to stop wolf reintroduction in the Yellowstone area from taking place. However, this effort was unsuccessful.

In January a total of 18 captured wolves were flown to the United States, four to be released in central Idaho and the rest destined for Yellowstone. The wolves lived in the acclimatization pens until March, getting used to their new surroundings. Biologists closely monitored the wolves during this time and food in the form of road-killed elk and deer was brought to the pens periodically. However, this had to be done at a distance because the policy was to minimize human contact with the wolves so that they would remain wild, and wary of humans. During this time the wolves in each of the three pens seemed to be adjusting well to their new surroundings, so well, in fact, that they were often seen playing with one another. After ten weeks of acclimatization they were released into the park.

Above: A gray wolf pair crossing a stream. The dominant breeding couple, or alpha pair, is the centerpiece of the pack. They are also usually the only breeding pair.

Above: A lone wolf emerges from a stream. Wolves are strong swimmers, but they generally go in the water only when it is necessary, such as to cross a river or stream.

Through the spring and summer of 1995, the wolves were monitored in the park, and in May, one of the females gave birth to eight pups on private land near Red Lodge, Montana. When the female's mate was illegally killed, the group was moved back into Yellowstone and later released inside the park, but by November, they, along with other wolves, were living in the Shoshone National Forest in Idaho. During the spring of 1996, it was observed that this same female, now with a new mate, gave birth to four more pups. In April 1996, the US Fish & Wildlife Service introduced an additional 17 wolves, captured in January in British Columbia, into Yellowstone and adjacent areas. By 1997, these wolves have formed into eight packs.

But this was only the beginning. Wolves are not only wild animals, but they are wanderers by nature. The wolf packs did not recognize the boundaries of the national park, so US Fish & Wildlife had the delicate and difficult task of monitoring their movements and controlling any illegal predation —

Above: The face of the gray wolf. The renowned naturalist and painter John James Audubon is best known for his work with birds of North America, but he also turned his attention to the wolf, citing its "strength, agility, and cunning."

Above: While Audubon recognized the adversarial nature of the relations between humans and wolves, a century later Jack London portrayed the wolf as the embodiment of a universal wild spirit in such novels as *The Call of the Wild* and *White Fang.*

either wolves killing livestock or humans killing wolves. Indeed, some of the wolves did leave the park, and some of these did prey on livestock. Meanwhile, another pack from northern Montana moved into the same area and began killing livestock. Under the terms of the reintroduction plan, US Fish and Wildlife Officers shot the adults, but they captured the pups and placed them into the acclimation pens with the two adults from Yellowstone. Although the Yellowstone wolf restoration effort did not need additional wolves to assure its success, biologists nonetheless made the decision to add these pups to the program, instead of leaving them to die on their own. These 12 wolves were then released in the spring of 1997.

Most of the packs remained within the park, and by 1997, there were 52 wolves inhabiting the Yellowstone area, including 13 wolves in captivity awaiting release, 35 free ranging wolves that could be monitored and four that could not be tracked. The overall success of the wolf reintroduction program,

Above and opposite: A lone wolf on the move in the dead of winter. The gray wolf is perfectly suited for such an environment. His thick coat keeps him warm, and the deep snow forces his prey to move more slowly, and to leave tracks.

especially as breeding occurred and new pups joined the packs, suggested that moving wolves from Canada to the United States would no longer be necessary to meet the goals of the wolf reintroduction program. The wolves in the Yellowstone area are doing far better at producing offspring than many experts had expected they would during the first years of wolf reintroduction. It also turned out that carcasses left by wolves, along with the wolves' intolerance for the presence of coyotes in their territory, would benefit other species, because wolves often cannot devour a kill at one time, so a partially eaten carcass may be left unattended by wolves between feedings. This offers an excellent opportunity for scavengers, from grizzly bears to magpies, to obtain a free meal.

Wolf recovery continues to be a polarized and controversial process. Attitudes are often based on inaccurate information, making wolf management perhaps more difficult than any other wildlife management program.

Above: A gray wolf high in the Rocky Mountains. In the last few years of the twentieth century, wolves have made history in this region.

Above: Descendants of Canadian wolves that took up residence in northwestern Montana continue to expand their range southward. They have begun to interact with wolves that were introduced into Yellowstone in the early 1990s.

Some conservationists seriously underestimate the potential danger wolves pose to livestock, while people who disagree with reintroduction fear that wolves will attack people. In fact, while wolves will attack livestock, they generally avoid humans. There are no verified reports of healthy wolves ever seriously injuring a human in North America in the twentieth century.

The restoration of gray wolves to natural environments from which they were so ruthlessly eradicated is an important milestone. It is also encouraging to see wolves reintroducing themselves into Glacier National Park. However, the management and control of restored wolf populations requires substantial planning and constant monitoring. It also requires that a balance be maintained between the concerns of ranchers and the long-term desire to round out the species balance in ecosystems such as Glacier and Yellowstone.

Above: The wolf's howl may be a greeting or a cheer to another wolf, but to humans, it echoes through the misty woods as a reminder that the deep northern forests are still wild.

Above: A gray wolf amid the aspen leaves on a cool, bright day in autumn. Soon the snows will come, the pack will be on the move and the winter breeding season will ensure a continuation of the cycle of life.

INDEX